Me and the Big C

One Woman's Journey through cancer's hardship, healing, and hope

By

Sue W Burris

Copyright © 2014 by by Sue W Burris
All rights reserved.
Book design by by Sue W Burris

No part of this book may be reproduced in any form or by any electronic or mechanical means including information storage and retrieval systems, without permission in writing from the author. The only exception is by a reviewer, who may quote short excerpts in a review.

Sue W Burris Books are available for order through Ingram Press Catalogues

In this publication, I have tried to recreate events, locales, and conversations from my memories of them. In order to maintain their anonymity, in some instances, I have changed names of individuals and places. I may have changed some identifying characteristics and details such as physical properties, occupations, and places of residence.

This book is not intended as a substitute for medical advice of physicians. The reader should regularly consult a physician in matters relating to his/her health and particularly with respect to any symptoms that may require diagnosis or medical attention.

Sue W Burris
Visit my website at www.suewburrisbooks.com
Printed in the United States of America
First Printing 2014
Published by Sojourn Publishing, LLC

ISBN: 978-1-62747-073-5
Ebook ISBN: 978-1-62747-074-2
LCN: Pending

Table of Contents

Dedication v
Introduction vii
Prologue xi

1. The Beginning 1
2. Chris's story 7
3. Bud and Ella 29
4. Suzy 39
5. Life Lessons from the Big C 51
6. Jan 57
7. Advice from a Cancer Pro 69
8. A Great Day 75

Epilogue 79
Acknowledgements 81
About the Author 83

Dedication

This book is dedicated to the memory of my dear sister, Janet Marie York, and to my 3 favorite cancer survivors—Bud and Ella Wilson, and my wonderful son, Chris Burris, all of whom inspired this book.

Also, to all my fellow cancer survivors everywhere—may the Lord continue to bless and keep you on your journey.

Introduction

As a health care provider for over 30 years, I still have a morbid fascination for wounds. Any wound. Decubitus ulcers, diabetic ulcers, venous ulcers, you name it, I am fascinated by the entire smelly, draining, gross lot of them. Through the years, I have debrided and given many wounds the opportunity to heal. For any wound to heal appropriately, the healing must occur from the inside outward. Many wounds, like people, may look intact from the outside, but have tunneling, putrid flesh still rotting on the inside. This book has been my healing wound, and, like a real wound, the real healing has finally occurred from the inside out.

My experiences with cancer began in the year 2000 with my son's illness, and ended ten years later with my sister's death from a rare and aggressive endometrial cancer. During the ensuing years, I always thought I would like to write a Christian based book to help others through similar experiences–not to be narcissistic, or get sympathy for my family, (for there are many families that have had similar experiences or worse), but to just simply help others by telling my family's story. I just knew I could write a book about it...someday.

Fast forward to the beginning of this year. As a recipient of the University of Tennessee's non-credit program e-mails, I noticed a short, one day course on writing by my mentor and now friend Tom Bird. During the winter, I attended one of his short courses and became hooked. Next came the course "Write Your Best Seller in a Weekend" in the month of May, and SOME DAY had finally arrived. I viewed the coursework prior to the course with a mixture of apprehension and false courage, and met with other authors to be for a common meal Thursday evening before the course began. The next day, on Friday, started one of the most intense and wonderful experiences I have ever had. I finally was able to put all my piecemeal, scattered, and sometimes very emotionally intense thoughts down in an organized fashion, and, by George, by the end of the weekend, a very rough draft of the book was finally done. A few more months of editing, adding a few more thoughts, a cover, and some other minor things, and voila! Here it is. Enjoy.

Prologue

This year in the United States alone over 1,665,540 people are estimated to be diagnosed with cancer. Overall mortality rates from the disease are approximately thirty two percent over a five year period. That means that over 585,720 people die yearly from cancer, making it America's second biggest killer after heart disease.

While heart disease often kills quickly, cancer is a chronic disease, and takes months, or often years, to kill its victims. Cancer is a non-discriminating killer. It cuts across all ages, genders, races, and socioeconomic scales with fierce intensity.

Even with millions of dollars funded by the government, private organizations, companies, and individuals, cancer wreaks havoc in this country with lost work days, astronomical medical expenses, and loss of life.

What can the individual do to prevent cancer? Sometimes nothing, but lifestyle choices and simply paying attention have been shown to make a huge difference in prevention and early detection of most types of cancer. Eating a clean diet high in fiber and free from preservatives (think fresh fruits and vegetables grown without toxic chemicals) protect the body against many common cancer types. Keeping drinking of alcohol to minimum recommended guidelines, regular exercise, and limiting exposure to environmental toxins are others. Tobacco use has been a documented carcinogen for over fifty years. JUST QUIT SMOKING AND USING ORAL TOBACCO!

Early detection is the key to survival in all types of cancer. Pay attention to your body. Get regular screenings, bloodwork, and mammograms. Make your health a priority. Here are the American Cancer Society's seven cancer warning signs:

1. Change in bowel or bladder habits.
2. A sore that does not heal.
3. Unusual bleeding or discharge.

4. Thickening or lump in the breast or elsewhere.
5. Indigestion or difficulty in swallowing.
6. Obvious change in wart or mole.
7. Nagging cough or hoarseness.

Cancer is often a familial disease. Consider genetic testing, and discuss prophylactic prevention with your healthcare provider if you happen to carry the gene for breast, ovarian, or other cancers. Genetic testing and counseling are available in most areas with large cancer treatment centers. Insurance companies are becoming more willing to reimburse for this important, and often lifesaving, information.

If you or your family member get the dreaded diagnosis, take heart. Go to the experts, get the best help you can, and hang in there. My prayers are with you and your family.

Chapter 1
The Beginning

"Farming is a good life, but not a good living."
~ Bud Wilson (my dad)

By way of introduction, I am a dyed-in-the-wool, bona fide, genuine, Tennessee farm girl. I grew up on a medium-sized family farm on the border of East and Middle Tennessee.

We were a happy family—Mom, Dad, and four kids—two boys, and two girls. All the time, but during summers especially, we worked hard and played hard. What happy memories—fishing and wading in the creek, making mud pies in the rain, catching baby frogs, riding around on the tailgate of Dad's old pickup truck—the stuff of *The Walton's* TV show. Ours was a strong family that worked well together because we had to, just to make ends meet and keep ourselves going.

My dad was the original equal-opportunity employer. If some work needed doing and you were in his family, you did it, and it really didn't matter what your gender was. Work was work, and that was that.

During my childhood and adolescence, I've helped haul hay, planted and hoed tobacco, fed baby dairy cows, fed hogs, snapped bushels of green beans, and mowed yards. As an adult, I am forever grateful to my parents for instilling a work ethic in me that is rare these days—don't finish until your work is done.

Ours was a close-knit family that played or worked together almost constantly. Our nearest neighbors were a half mile away—one group had no kids, and the others' kids were already grown, so we had our own neighborhood. Add to that a multitude of cousins who were in and out of our farmhouse all the time, and you can see that although my childhood wasn't perfect, it was close to it. If we had any troubles, they weren't readily apparent—in matters of health, especially.

After I left the family farm, I started school at the University of Tennessee. As a freshman, my dream was to become a doctor, but after some volunteer work at Children's hospital in Knoxville, and some encouragement from my mom, I started looking at careers in physical or occupational therapy. At that time, physical therapy jobs were more plentiful in small towns, and Tennessee had one school, and one school only, and that was in Memphis. While at UT, I met and became engaged to my forever guy, Mark. We got married and moved to Memphis two weeks later. Five years later, we had a PT degree (I say "we," because we said "I do," and I said, "Goodbye, I have to study"), two kids, an old historic house in a good neighborhood, a mortgage, and a dog and cat. Life was good and stayed good for a long time. When our youngest child started school, we opened our first physical therapy outpatient clinic, and owned and operated it for twenty-two years. I am now working on call and part time jobs, and the stress reduction is wonderful. Life is still good, even with its ups and downs. Here is my story:

With the dawn of a new millennium, our life began to change. My kids were teenagers, with my oldest in his first semester at college. Mom and Dad were retired, aging well, and enjoying life. Then the bomb dropped. First, my son was diagnosed with leukemia—not a rare type, but rare occurring in his age group. Next, two weeks later, my mother was diagnosed with breast cancer; me, two years later, with breast cancer, and my dad, three years later, with prostate cancer. Finally, at the end of the decade, my sister was diagnosed with a rare, aggressive type of uterine (endometrial) cancer, and died soon after her diagnosis.

We went from being family of the year to shell-shocked and worried within a ten-year time frame. What was wrong? As a family, we have tried to figure out why we've been bitten so hard by the cancer bug. In fact, it has been so bad that when our daughter was first engaged to be married, I said to my prospective son-in-law, "Son, are you sure you want to take a dip in our gene pool?" (He did). Was it the insecticides? DDT was popular in the 1970s. In fact, our family probably still has so many chemicals lurking around in our bodies that we could just blow on a bug and kill it at forty paces. How about the chemicals we used to refinish furniture? This was a hobby of mine and my mother's when I was a teen. Or maybe, as my geneticist said—just crappy genes. Even to the current time, we are still unsure of the external or internal causes for all our family's cancer. It really doesn't matter—what does matter is in the words of Paul Harvey ... the rest of the story.

Chapter 2
Chris's story

It's a great day to be alive.
~ Travis Tritt

It was almost the end of fall semester at the University of Tennessee for my son—the Monday after Thanksgiving to be exact. Chris had not been feeling well during the Thanksgiving break, and had been pretty lethargic. While trying to help his dad build an equipment shed, he had become weak and unable to lift. He had a slight fever, fatigue, and had lost some weight during his first semester away at college. He had, in fact, some of the classic signs of mononucleosis, I thought. "Son, when you get back to school on Monday, go to the student health clinic. Ask about getting some blood work. I think you have

Mono." Oh, if only it could have been mono! Later that day, about 3:00 PM, I got a call that Sunday school lessons always talk about. "What would you do if you got a call saying your child was _____ fill in the blank (killed in a wreck, found dead from suicide, found to have a terminal disease)?"

The conversation with the health clinic doctor went something like this:

"Mrs. Burris?"

"Yes."

"This is Doctor Lyle from UT Health Clinic. Is your husband with you?"

"No, he is out of the office." *What the heck is wrong, this can't be good.*

"Are you sitting down?"

"Yes, okay, I am now." *Oh, dear God, is Chris dead? Just please tell me what it is already!*

"I am on the way to the hospital with your son—he has leukemia. You need to come to UT hospital as soon as possible."

With my voice shaking, I said, "Of course. We're on our way."

I hung up the phone and frantically called my husband, and then our teenage daughter, telling her to lock up the house and get to my office as soon as possible, since her brother had a medical emergency.

Before the rest of the family got to my office, my son called back, and with his voice breaking, said, "Mom, why is this happening to me?"

I answered, "I don't know, Buddy, but hang in there, we are on our way, and we will be there as quick as we can." My heart was breaking, and even the relatively short 70 mile drive felt like an eternity.

We jumped in our Suburban and drove like madmen to the hospital, making the normally one and one half hour drive in 45-50 minutes, crying and praying all the way. When we arrived at the hospital, I literally ran into the building frantically searching for someone to tell us where our son was. We found him on the cancer ward, on the sixth floor. As we walked onto the hospital floor searching for him, a large, framed print with these words greeted us:

What Cancer Cannot Do
Cancer is so limited ...
It cannot cripple love.
It cannot shatter hope.
It cannot corrode faith.

It cannot eat away peace.
It cannot destroy confidence.
It cannot kill friendship.
It cannot shut out memories.
It cannot silence courage.
It cannot reduce eternal life.
It cannot quench the Spirit.
Author Unknown

During the drive up, we had called our families and a couple of dear close friends to ask them to pray for our son. Within just hours of when we arrived at the hospital, we had some really wonderful things happen.

Our son had a male nurse, who very patiently sat with him and watched him carefully until we got there. The physician from the student health center met us in a short time and filled us in on the medical aspects of our son's situation and said, "I'm praying for you." We found out later that our son's condition was serious, but not critical, but at that time, we thought he could easily die. As a mother, that is something you never expect or want to hear—it is much less painful and more in the natural order of things for children to outlive their parents. I just kept imagining my son dying—I was so upset, I couldn't eat or even begin to think about sleeping. I just wanted to hold him close and never let him go. I was frightened out of my wits, and almost out of my good sense.

We have a wonderful church family, and before the evening was over, Chris's best friend, a couple of his youth leaders, and our minister and his wife arrived. What a welcome sight they were! They prayed with us and gave an incredible amount of support to us and our son. Chris met privately with our minister, Mitchell, for a while and voiced some concerns to him, and gained some additional insight and support from him at a time that he needed it the most.

Tests started about the time we got to the hospital—blood work, x-rays, and near midnight that night, a CT scan. When you have leukemia, abdominal organs, particularly the liver and spleen, become overwhelmed with trying to filter out all the immature white blood cells, so in advanced disease, these organs begin to swell. CT scans are given to see the extent of swelling and/or organ involvement. Chris was on the way to the scanner in the bowels of UT hospital. I was still in "stick right by his side and never let him go mode," so I walked to the scanner with him. To this day, both of us swear we heard a cat meow, thus the reason for the name CAT scan. That was one of the first times we were able to laugh, and it felt good.

Also included in the testing was blood work drawn from his sister for evaluating her for a donor search for a possible bone marrow transplant, which was, and still is, the only known cure for leukemia. We were told that the best chance for a donor would be a full-blooded sibling of the patient, and since we only have two children, our daughter was his best choice. At the time, we were told that there are six factors looked at for matching for bone marrow transplantation, and that they can only do the transplant if four or five or more factors match. As a single sibling, the chances were only 25 percent that our daughter would be even a partial match. Blessings occurred again when within the next day or two, we found our daughter was a perfect 6/6 match for her brother. The Lord is good. A nonrelated bone marrow donor search can last up to six months and cost thousands of dollars, so we had this as an ace in the hole.

Me and the Big C

Interestingly, as my daughter and I were in the lab that first terrible evening, God sent the first of many prayer warrior angels into our path. We must have just looked devastated (of course we were!), and this particular lady gently asked why we were at the hospital. "We just found out our son has leukemia."

"You know," she said, "five years ago, my son was rappelling and suffered a bad fall, injuring his head. His doctors told us with the brain damage he suffered, he would likely be a vegetable. I just need you to know what God can do. Our son will graduate from college in a few weeks, and he's doing fine. Can I put you on our church's prayer chain?"

What a comfort! What a blessing! "Of course, you can put us on your prayer chain. Thank you so much!"

The next day went by in a blur of activity. A port-a-cath was put in for chemo therapy. More tests and blood work were done and drawn. At least thirty family, friends, and church family came and visited with us in the waiting room, and prayed with and for us.

After a while, memories fade, but one particular visitor sticks out in my mind. A special young man, my sister-in-law's nephew, whom I refer to as my nephew-in-law, heard the news and drove down from Sevierville to see us. Matthew had lost his mother three years before from metastatic breast cancer, and before he left, he gave me a fierce hug, and with tears in his eyes, told me he would be praying. He knew and shared the hurt that he knew we were feeling.

After lots of testing and blood work, we were waiting for the doctor, an oncologist and hematologist from UT Medical Center. In the meantime, a dear family friend and physician called and talked to me, giving me one of the best pieces of advice I had heard in a long time. "Before you decide on treatment, make SURE you nail down a correct diagnosis—otherwise you may get the wrong treatment regimen." GREAT advice! It wasn't too long until the oncologist came in and gave us the news. Good news, as it turned out. Chris had one of the four major types of leukemia, chronic myeloid, which has a much better outlook that the more acute types. Still though, research at that time showed that the average life expectancy for CML was only three to five years. Doing some quick math, I determined that the oldest my son could live to be was twenty-three years old. "God, "I prayed, "how can I stand this? He is such a vital part of our family, how can I live without him?" My heart was just crushed.

On the evening Chris was admitted to the hospital, there was no sleeping to be had. First of all, hospital chairs are about as comfortable as a bed of nails, and secondly, we were all just too upset to sleep. Around 5 o'clock the next morning, Chris was finally sleeping, and I couldn't, so I just wandered around the hospital waiting room. I sat down in a chair, and the tears finally came—not just regular tears, but the huge, heaving sobs of a mom with uncontrollable grief—first grief, and then rage at circumstances that I couldn't control.

With your children, as a mother, your first instinct is to make everything better. Well, this was a boo-boo that couldn't be fixed. It was, as the children's book says, an awful, no good, terrible day.

Even though my son still had a cancer diagnosis, we found out that his type of cancer could be treated with oral medication. The side effects were pretty much lousy, especially for a young person Chris's age. Flu-like symptoms, fatigue, and bone aches didn't sound pretty, but it would buy him some time. In the meantime, we were asked to travel to a large teaching hospital in a nearby city which was one of the few facilities in the state that were able to perform bone marrow transplants, to be evaluated for bone marrow transplantation. Our experience at the teaching hospital was highly negative. We arrived around the first of December, and the office staff seemed more interested in putting up Christmas decorations than giving time to a family with a new diagnosis that was devastating. The nursing staff filling in didn't know how to run the equipment, and the doctor was negative. We left there more hopeless than we were when we came. It was so discouraging. It was, in fact, horrible. My son said, "Mom, do we have to stay there?" To which my reply was, "No, we will find another place and go anywhere you want to, Son." We waited a few days, and friends and family were giving us information from the internet that had some info on a new drug, called STl 571, that was having remarkable results. The drug, in fact, was developed by a researcher from the University of Oregon, and was in third stage clinical trials all across the country. It was having fabulous results, and was allowing people with CML to live normal lives without the side effects of regular chemo drugs, no hair loss, and little nausea and fatigue. It was the first of a new generation of drugs that targeted just the cancer, not all fast-growing cells in the body, and was making headlines. Our doctor in Knoxville had briefly mentioned the drug, but after we learned about it, we began doing some intensive research into it to see if there were any clinical trials available in our area.

God does some crazy wonderful things. One afternoon, our secretary had to leave our private practice physical therapy clinic because of a stomach virus. It was a non-clinic day, and so I was able to sit and answer the phone. Thankfully, it was quiet, so I was able to begin calling on a list of facilities that offered clinical trials on the new drug. I talked or left messages at facilities in Boston, Memphis, and at MD Anderson Cancer center in Houston, Texas. Later that evening, at home, the research nurse in the leukemia department at MD Anderson, Mary Anne, called me back. We talked about Chris's case, the new drug, and third stage clinical trials. Mary Anne explained to me that in third stage trials, the patient would either get the new drug, or a control drug in a blind controlled study. Then I asked her, "Do you have kids?"

"Yes," she said. "In fact, my son is turning nineteen today."

"If this were your kid, what would you do?"

"I would get him this drug."

We talked for a short time longer about a possible trial available in the Memphis area, I thanked her, and hung up.

Prayers are often answered by working through angels here on earth, and Mary Anne turned out to be ours. The next morning at work, I received a phone call from her. "Sue, I thought about your son on my way home last night, and I've spoken with the doctor this morning. If you can get your son down here before his spleen and liver go down, we will get him in a trial for more advanced disease and we will get him on this drug." Modern-day miracles really do happen, and this was one. I said, "Let me know when and where, and we will be there." An appointment was made for Monday, only two and a half days away.

The next few hours went by in a flurry of planning, getting flight arrangements made, and getting medical records transferred. "HOUSTON, WE HAVE A PROBLEM, AND WE'RE COMING DOWN." Flight arrangements turned out to be a blessing, and the first of many, many, wonderful things that happened to us during Chris's cancer experience. My husband Mark is a pilot, and one of his pilot friends and a local businessman teamed up and chartered a private jet to take us to Houston, leaving directly from our little Tennessee town and going straight to Hobby airport in Houston, Texas. This was a good thing, since with leukemia, the immune system is so depressed that any kind of viral or bacterial infection is easy to catch. In leukemia, the blood is so full of immature white blood cells that the mature ones can't do their jobs of protecting the body against disease, so a private flight without other passengers was a godsend.

We arrived in Houston on a Sunday afternoon, got settled in the motel, and were ready for the next morning's round of appointments beginning at 7:00 AM. One of the most wonderful things about MD Anderson is the sense of hope that you get when you walk in that building. The sense is *if your cancer can be beat, you have come to the right place.* Our day began with a visit to a social worker, and then we went up to the blood borne cancer floor. You see, MD Anderson is so big that they devote a floor to each kind or group of cancers—breast cancer has one floor, prostate another, blood borne cancers another, and so on. Anyway, when we arrived at our floor, the place was packed. It seems that Monday is new patient day, and most of the doctors had been gone to a seminar in San Francisco the week before, so people with cancer were everywhere. Everywhere you looked, there was someone bald, with tubes hanging everywhere, or just looking gravely ill. It was a humbling and at the same time terrifying experience. I wanted to scream, "Please just let us see the doctor! Can't you see my son may die?!" At the same time, I realized everyone in that room was in the same boat we were. We just had to be patient and wait our turn. Also, many of the people we met were very gravely ill, and they all had stories. There was the young woman that found out she had leukemia during her pregnancy, and the man who told us if he hadn't been diagnosed when he was that he would have been dead in two weeks. There were people in that waiting room from all over the country and all over the world. One gentleman we met on that first trip asked us if he could put us on the prayer chain at his men's weekly prayer breakfast. Of course, we said yes. We had contact with that gentleman for years after that initial contact. God is so good, and put so many wonderful people in our lives that we really needed to meet and hear for hope and inspiration.

By the end of that day, we had finally seen the doctor. We spent a total of twelve hours in the facility by the time we were through, and were signed up to begin getting the drug starting the next day. STI 571 was fast-tracked through the FDA because of such positive results, and became commercially available about six months after the clinical trial. Because the medicine was in clinical trials, we were also asked to see a bone marrow transplant doctor, because that was still the only known cure for the disease at that time, and still is. The downside to a bone marrow transplant, however, is that there is about a 50 percent, and only a 50 percent, survival rate, and that is at the best facilities. The rate goes down from there. So ... you get well or you die. There were a lot of reasons I didn't want to do this, but mainly, at the time, I felt my son's condition was so weakened that he wouldn't survive the ordeal. You see, for a bone marrow transplant to occur, first, the patient's own bone marrow has to be destroyed, and the immune system has to be taken down to ground zero. In other words, before the transplant, the immune system has to be destroyed so the new marrow, in this case from Chris's sister, could grow without rejection. So this, I felt, was not the best option for us. We wanted that drug. And, the next day, we got it.

The first dose of the drug was given on a Tuesday night, and we were able to leave Houston on a Wednesday. On Tuesday, Chris also had his port-a-cath removed, since it was leaking, and he was doing oral meds anyway. We were to return to Houston in March and get a recheck of everything, including a very painful and soreness-inducing bone marrow aspiration. We were to get weekly blood work to see how Chris's white counts were doing. I should add here that if a normal person has an infection, the flu, or something like that, white counts in blood work go up to the 12,000 range. Medical providers begin to suspect leukemia at a level of about 20,000. At the beginning of his disease, Chris's counts were 320,000, well off the scale at a typical doctor's office. He was a sick, a very sick, boy.

When we returned home, we got blood work every week. It was almost like a game... are they going to fall in half again? The first week, it went down by half, the second week down to about 75,000, and within just a few months, the blood counts were within normal ranges. My boy was getting better!! What a great drug!

When you have a child (in this case young adult) with a possibly terminal illness, you become an instant helicopter mom. Son, do you feel okay? Son, is there anything I can get for you? Are you feeling feverish, or nauseated? What could you eat today? And on and on and on. Of course, Chris was a young man—with emphasis on the word MAN—and as anyone his age would do, he finally tired of my constant hovering. "Mom, would you just leave me alone?" he shouted. "Listen, Buddy, you scared me so bad, you are lucky you are sleeping by yourself!" I hollered back. He just looked at me and shook his head. After that, I tried to back off and he tried to be patient, and we got along a lot better. This all leads me to say this: Cancer is dang stressful. It is an emotional land mine, can destroy relationships, —and don't even get me started on the money. Cancer treatment is the most expensive medical treatment out there. Drugs such as the one Chris is on may run up to $8000-$10,000 per month. Bone marrow transplants run about a half million to a million dollars with the prep, transplant itself, and follow-up. If you don't have insurance or have inadequate insurance, a family can be in financial ruin from cancer treatment—and be in it quick. Yes, there are resources out there, but they are often limited, and are on a first-come-first-served basis. It is no wonder families with a cancer patient fall apart just from financial worries alone. To say cancer is stressful on a lot of fronts—emotional, financial, physical—is a huge understatement.

It is devastating. It is hard. It is hell. But it is survivable, with a strong faith, a lot of prayer, and good medicine.

Our son has never been able to sit still, and sitting in the house during bad weather in January just watching TV between community college classes was just not going to do. He asked Mark and me what we thought about him getting a job, and we said sure, a light part-time job would be great. Well, the next thing we knew he had a job all right. He was hired in a diesel shop as an apprentice mechanic, on his feet for hours a day repairing heavy equipment. REALLY? This is your idea of light work? As I was fussing about his choice at my church, an older lady called me over. This lady was a cancer survivor, a life survivor, and tough as nails. She looked right at me and said, "Honey (remember we are Tennesseans), let him work, it will take his mind off the cancer." I took that to heart and continued to work throughout my own cancer treatments, partially because I had my own business and had to, but mostly to keep my mind off me, and keep mentally sane. It works, and if I am asked to pass out advice about what to do with a diagnosis of cancer, I will always say, "Work as long as you can." I think it keeps you physically and emotionally much healthier, and certainly helps with financial considerations, especially if your insurance is through your employer. Good advice from a dear lady with a degree from the school of hard knocks. Make that great advice.

With the clinical trial, though, came a lot of anxiety. What if the drug stops working? What about the side effects? What if we made the wrong decision and he really does need a bone marrow transplant? This anxiety tortured me for about six months. I couldn't sleep, didn't eat particularly well, and, just in general, did not take really good care of myself. Then, about six months out, I was praying, like normal, for Chris's complete healing, and I finally had a deep conviction that my son would be okay no matter what the outcome. You see, even if my son died, as a believing Christian, he would continue to live on in a wonderful place, which I could only imagine. There was nothing to fear really, and I just needed to remember the Bible verse that I had been drawn to since college: Matthew 6:34, "Therefore do not worry about tomorrow, for tomorrow will worry about itself.

Each day has enough trouble of its own." You see, each day brings its own joy, and sometimes its own sorrow. Living in the moment is especially important when your days may be numbered. In fact, all of our days are numbered, aren't they? This was the first of many important truths that I learned through the first cancer experience.

At this writing, my son is a thirteen-year cancer survivor. Though he has to continue with oral medication, and likely will for the rest of his life, he has graduated college (twice), gotten married, and has just had his first child. He works every day and generally is just one of the good guys. He has learned a lot from his cancer experience, and wants to survive to be a great dad to his new little girl. My son is a walking answered prayer, and could easily be a model for a *Life is Good* tee shirt. Life is good, and so is God.

Chapter 3
Bud and Ella

"Her children arise and call her blessed."
~ Proverbs 31

My family had just arrived back from Houston on a late flight Wednesday evening. The next morning as I was preparing for work, I heard a car drive up in the driveway. Thinking it was odd to have such an early visitor, I was surprised to see my mom and dad exiting their car. As they walked in the door, I remember thinking, *this can't be good*. That thought, like so many of my premonitions, was, unfortunately, correct. You see, Mom announced to me that morning that she had breast cancer, and she was on her way with my dad to Knoxville to see an oncologist for treatment options. "Oh my gosh, not again. Lord, this can't be happening! I may lose my son and my mother, too? Nooooooo!" I told our teenage daughter, foolishly, I shouldn't have upset her like that before school, but I think I was just in shock. Another day or two went by and Mom had elected to schedule a modified radical mastectomy the day after Christmas. Let me tell you, celebrating the birth of Christ is hard when you are even doubting your own faith. Christmas was bittersweet that year; with me wanting to make it special and memorable, but also realizing that by the next year, we could possibly be without two beloved family members, was just about more than I could bear. I went through all the motions—put up the tree, planned the dinners, decorated the house, all the while working, running a business, and taking care of my family (Chris had moved back home and elected to go to a local community college while he was recuperating, and I just breathed a sigh of relief to have him back home again.) Like so many times in my life, I went onto auto pilot...just put on a brave face, keep the family together, make good decisions, keep it together girl. I found out later just how harmful that can be.

Mom's surgery was the day after Christmas at an older hospital in downtown Knoxville. A word to the wise... never have surgery, unless you just have to, around a major holiday. There are skeleton crews working, and care is just not as good. Anyway, I was able to tear myself away from my sick boy for an overnight stay in the hospital with Mom. My sister had been with her earlier in the day, and I was able to trade out and stay overnight. The surgery went fine. There was some soreness, with the aggravation of drain tubes, but the especially good news was that lymph nodes were negative. Yeaaaaaa! No more intervention. Surgery and home. At last some super good news. Mom would be okay.

When my mom had her mastectomy, my Dad and I stayed with her during her postsurgical night. It was the day after Christmas and before New Year's, so the lights and Christmas decorations in downtown Knoxville were still up, bright and pretty. Well, my dad was determined for my mom to see the lights, post-op or not. As kids, we used to travel around during the Christmas season and look at beautifully decorated homes in our small town. Mom loved it and so did we. So we pulled her IV pole over, unlocked the bed, and rolled her right in front of the window to see several beautifully decorated Christmas trees on top of a downtown bank. She was less than impressed, but they were beautiful, and reminded us that Christmas is about healing, and God's perfect gift.

My mother is of a generation where women quietly endured and really just didn't make a big deal of anything, no matter how serious. She made it through the surgery and recovery like a champ.

It is a funny thing about women who seem strong, though. We are tough on the outside and scared, upset, and crying on the inside. What seems tough on the exterior is just a façade—a sometimes very physically and emotionally unhealthy façade that looks good on the outside but just crumbles away on the interior. Another of the many lessons cancer has taught me is tough is not always the best thing to be. It is NOT a sign of weakness to ask for help, depend on others, or not try to do everything by yourself. Most people, even strangers, are glad to help, and, indeed, one of the best things you can do for your friends and loved ones is to allow them the empowerment of being able to do something productive to help.

When I was able to sit with my Mom, even though I was overwhelmed with the sometimes crushing responsibilities of my son, my job, and overcoming my own distraught emotional state, I was empowered by being able to do **something.** As someone used to being a caretaker, it comes very naturally to me to help people, either loved ones or strangers. But when I am the one facing the sharp side of that needle, it is a very different story. When you are the sick person, unable even to turn over in bed without becoming sick, it is a very humbling experience to ask for help, and indeed, even accept it from close family members. It is tempting to transfer the rage and anger you feel toward the disease to the very people who want to help you the most. Even though my mom didn't express it, I know she felt the same way. As a nurse with a career spanning almost forty years, it did not come second nature to her to ask for help either.

As a friend or family member of someone diagnosed with cancer, one of the best things you can do is just shut up and listen. Don't try to say everything will be okay, what you've heard about the latest successful treatments, or, heaven forbid, that somebody else you know has suffered and died from the same type of cancer (and yes, people really do this—incredible, I know). What a family member or loved one really wants to hear when he or she has gotten the cancer diagnosis is this—I love you. I will do anything for you within my power to get you good and appropriate treatment, and, what can I do to help? You have one hundred percent of my support, and I have your back. If you know of a cancer survivor who is doing well with the same disease, it is certainly time to introduce this person to your family member with cancer.

Here are some things not to say: "Just let me know what I can do" (don't depend on a cancer patient to remember to call you—he or she is too busy just trying to survive). A better option might be… "Your grass looks like it needs mowing. Would it be okay if I came over Thursday afternoon to take care of it?" Instead of "I'll fix you dinner sometime." How about, "Our young couple's group at church would like to bring you dinner once a week. What day of the week is your busiest? We could bring it then if you like." Or my favorite classic, "I really like your hat. Where did you get it? I would love to wear something like that on days I don't want to fix my hair." Need I say more about tactless comments? All any cancer patient wants to know is people care. All friends and family really need to do is show the cancer patient how much they do care. Don't worry about offending someone or saying just the right words of wisdom, just hug them and tell them they are in your prayers, and you love them. Simple, but oh so important to the emotional stability and hope of your friends or family with cancer.

Family members really have it rough. Especially with cancer diagnoses that look like they will not have a good outcome, there may be a really rough road ahead. The cancer patient, in some ways, has it easier than the family. If it looks like death is imminent, yes, there is some emotional and physical discomfort for the patient, but eventually, there has to be peace made with the inevitability of your own demise. For the family, however, it is a different story. Families have to watch and agonize over the dying process. Sometimes, death from cancer can be really ugly, with gradual or sudden decline and eventual loss of all functions. Families have to watch it happen. It is much harder for a family to accept the suffering of a loved one that very often goes with the cancer process. Elizabeth Kubler Ross listed the steps in the dying process, with the final one being acceptance. Believe me when I say acceptance is hard, even nearly impossible, for families. So, when you are with a cancer patient, be very aware of the family also, because like so many long-term diseases, cancer is a **family** disease. Be supportive of the entire group, not just the patient. You will never know how much it is appreciated.

Mom is now a thirteen-year survivor, having also survived joint replacement, a stroke, and ongoing responsibilities as major caregiver for my dad. She is a trooper, and I want to be just like her when I grow up. God has blessed me with a wonderful mother.

My dad has also suffered from a reproductive cancer. As with many men in their seventies, a small area of cancer was found on Dad's prostate gland two to three years before treatment was begun. The medical term for this is "watchful waiting," which means the situation may or may not require any intervention or treatment, but is carefully monitored. In Dad's case, his treatment consisted of radioactive seeding of the prostate to get rid of cancer cells. The treatment was successful in killing the cancer, and Dad is now an eleven year survivor. He is one tough dude. In addition to cancer, he has lived through removal of a giant (size of a woman's fist) benign brain tumor, massive pulmonary embolus (blood clot in the lung), diabetes, and short term memory loss. God love him, he is still able to walk, drive, and eat. Again, God is so good, all the time.

Chapter 4
Suzy

"For the joy of the Lord is your Strength."
~ Nehemiah 8:10

Here's my story. If you are beginning to think my family has been hit with the cancer stick, you are so right. My story begins two short years after my son's. Again in the latter part of the year, again during the holidays, on December fifth, the day before my mom's birthday. A couple of weeks earlier, during a shower, I had noticed a lump in my left breast. This was no big deal really, I have fibrocystic disease, and lumps come and lumps go. But this one didn't go. This one came and stayed. It was hard, and it was painless. Let me just say that I was keeping my mammograms up, especially since my Mom's experience. It was, in fact, time for me to get one. So, instead of getting it locally, I decided to go to my mom's doctor in Knoxville for evaluation. To their credit, when I called with my complaint, the Knoxville Comprehensive breast center got me in for an appointment within a couple of days. Foolishly, I thought I had to schedule this around my work, so I didn't go as soon as I should have. When I got there, I went through the mammogram and was called back for an ultrasound. This is never a good sign. If you are called for an ultrasound, something is up. It may not always be bad, but it could be. The doctor came in and did my ultrasound. Again, not a good sign. Usually, the technicians will do the ultrasound. I sat up on the bed, the doctor took a deep breath, and said, "You have breast cancer." All I could say was, "Well," as in, "Oh, well." Nothing like this is unusual in my family, especially lately. I put my clothes back on, made an appointment for later in the week, and jumped in my truck and headed home. Again, on auto pilot. My husband called. I didn't answer. I really didn't want to give him the news, period, much less over the phone. I don't remember anything about the drive home except getting home and going in. My husband was worried and aggravated that I hadn't called him back. All I could say is, "Honey, I have breast cancer, and I didn't want to tell you over the phone."

He looked like I just hit him in the face. "I am so sorry. I had no idea you would get bad news."

Me either. I was the strong one of the family, remember? The Enjoli woman. Remember the old jingle, "I can bring home the bacon, fry it up in the pan, and never, never let you forget you're a man." Yeah, right. The next few months would show me how strong I wasn't, but it would also send me on a growth journey that I loathed at the time, but looking back was one of the best things that ever happened to me.

When I was diagnosed with breast cancer, both of our kids were in college, Chris at Tennessee Tech University, and Beki at Middle Tennessee State in Murfreesboro. Because they were both about to go into finals week, Mark and I (mostly me) made the decision that it would be best to wait and tell them about the diagnosis until after they finished their semester tests. Mark found out when Chris's tests were finished and drove to the college, and told him in person. Chris's roommate and our daughter were dating (it stuck, they are now married with two children), and Ivy requested to be there when we told Beki to support her. This is a sign of a fine young man, and I really respected him for this. Anyhow, Beki was told, and typically tough as a hickory nut, one single tear slid down her cheek. She grew up some more that day—she was sixteen when her brother was diagnosed, so she had to grow up fast and tough, but cancer has made a real difference in her life. She is one of the kindest, most compassionate young women I know. She's also a go-getter, and you can come to your own conclusions when I tell you that her brother's nickname for her is "The Boss." I will just leave it at that.

When I was first diagnosed with breast cancer, my husband went into full-fledged take-charge and beat-the-heck-out-of-it mode. I know he was scared to death, and his way of dealing with it was to control every situation down to the very last detail. We were going to Houston because they were the best, and BY GOSH, if we had to stay in Houston over Christmas, we just would, and to heck with the rest of the family or the celebration. Well, Christmas is a big day for me, full of family, good food, and lots of laughter. In all my years, I had never been away from my family for Christmas, and I was hell-bent that we were going to celebrate it in Tennessee. We had a heated discussion about it. I WAS going to get my way, and WE WERE going to be in Tennessee for Christmas. End of story. Bless our son's heart, he finally ran intervention with his dad, and we calmed down as a couple and a family. It was hard, irritating, and scary, all rolled into one. There is nothing fun about cancer.

Every cancer patient needs a good mentor, and God brought me a great one. Denise is a mother of four boys who hunt, fish, and four-wheel, and just generally have a good time being manly men. Denise is also a breast cancer survivor and had cancer a few years before me. I met Denise through a mutual family member, and she gave me a piece of advice I never forgot. Good advice for strong women. The advice was, "its okay to let yourself cry over a cancer diagnosis, but don't let yourself cry for more than one day at a time. That is not okay."

"Thanks, Denise." I didn't.

The next few days were filled with doctor's appointments, tests, and planning treatment regimens. I found out, at age forty-four, that most every doctor's office in the country considered chemotherapy a must, because of my age and the size of my cancer. Since Chris was going to Houston, we just made it a family affair and headed out to Texas. Four family members, luggage, and a cooler in a small ladies' sized pickup truck for one thousand miles made for quite a cramped trip, but I loved the people I was with. Houston was quite an experience. First of all, the breast cancer center was incredibly busy! It was packed. We spoke with a nurse practitioner, the doctor, and others before we settled on a treatment regimen. I got a copy of the protocol and found that my physicians in Knoxville had no problem with using MD Anderson's protocol for chemo, so I could receive my chemo locally, and then just call Anderson for consultation if need be. Much to my dismay, not only did the folks at MD Anderson agree that I needed chemo, they gave a much more aggressive regimen that the providers in Knoxville did. It was tough. Also, rather than removing my breast first, and then receiving chemo, the providers at Anderson insisted on giving chemo therapy prior to any surgery. As the nurse practitioner so eloquently put it, "If you don't do this, it could cost you your life." Neo adjuvant therapy they called it. I didn't like it. My thoughts were if your breast is going to kill you, then for Pete's sake, cut it off and throw it away. Oh, the doctor gave me breast preserving options. It has been my observation, though, that there are two camps of women with breast cancer—those who will preserve their breasts if at all possible, and those who say, "Get this thing the heck off me and get it off now, and take the other one while you are at it!" I fell in the latter camp, so the idea of keeping my diseased breast really worried me. I wanted it off, and yesterday would have been not soon enough. As it worked out, though, my chemo worked, and worked well. The lump literally shrunk week by week. I was so excited, I just wanted to show everyone. "Here, feel my breast ... see how much smaller the lump is?!"

It took a couple of rounds of chemo before my hair began to come out. Fortunately, mine did not come out in big clumps, but just several hairs at a time. Hair was everywhere—on my pillow, in the sink, in the shower—I even had to start wearing a bandana so I wouldn't get hair in our food when I was cooking. During Chris's cancer experience someone had told us the best thing to do when your hair started coming out was to just shave it. With Mark's help, we cut my hair really short, and then later, he helped me get rid of the rest of it. At the end of about six weeks of treatments, I was totally bald. Speaking of bald … it really bothered me more than I thought it would to lose my hair. Without hair, man, we women are just ugly. I can also say, even though I met women who loved theirs, there was no such thing as a comfortable wig for me. They are hot, scratchy, and uncomfortable. I would wear mine at work. (Really, do you want YOUR physical therapist to be bald?) And then at home off it would come, with a bandana or soft hat to cover my bald head. After the first round of chemo, my hair grew back slightly, and then with the second round, I lost ALL my hair, including my eyebrows and eyelashes. I was hairless for almost an entire year. I found that hair on your head and face has several essential functions, with the most important one being keeping you from freezing to death. My head and entire body were just freezing most of the time. Eyebrows and eyelashes keep stuff out of your eyes. I don't know how animals like turtles do it. I was constantly rubbing my eyes to get stuff out of them. Even though hair loss bothered me a lot, it doesn't faze some women. I had a good friend that ordered in pizza and had a head shaving party with her kids when she began losing her hair. She had a great time, and so did they. She survived, by the way, I think in part to her great attitude.

Here was our schedule: a weekly trip to Knoxville for twelve weeks. Leave every Friday at lunch, eat, drive to Knoxville to chemo, and return home at supper time. I will have to insert something here. Never, not one time, was I left by myself in chemo, and I am so thankful. My wonderful husband, mom, dad, and daughter were with me every step of the way. I am blessed with a supportive family, and at no time in my life did I ever need them any more than I did during my cancer experience. They were with me and encouraged me through every single treatment session. I love them all so much. After the twelve weeks were over. I had a brief rest, and then my schedule was for a cocktail of three drugs given once a week every three weeks. The last four treatments were pure hell. I would go get a treatment, go home, or, for the last three treatments, to our local hospital to get fluids, and start throwing up. This lasted for forty-eight hours, period. It didn't matter what drugs I had, I had to endure nonstop vomiting during this time frame. Anticipating this was not good. I would cry, cuss, and want to run away. It was awful, and there was no way of sugarcoating it. The medicines were so strong, they were on your breath and in your skin for all three weeks between treatments. Mosquitos wouldn't touch you. Even a long-standing fungal infection in my big toe was resolved with chemo. Rough stuff. But thankfully, I survived it. If you have cancer, I would not recommend looking at the possible side effects of the drugs you are taking. Mine included: kidney damage, heart valve damage, and leukemia. (Wasn't one enough?) In addition, with every treatment, there was a risk of having a severe allergic reaction to the drugs, which could possibly put you into anaphylatic shock. Scary stuff. Here's the thing, though: Having a significant life-threatening disease can teach you about life in a way that a library full of books could never even begin to. Just keep reading.

Chapter 5
Life Lessons from the Big C

What I learned from cancer treatment:

1. God is Good, and so are family, friends, and community
2. When you have cancer, you experience prejudice, maybe for the first time in your life. If you are bald and sick, people have a tendency to write you off. Adults won't look at you, and kids stare. It is totally weird.
3. You can't control everything. Actually, you can't control anything. Life happens. It doesn't matter how healthy you are, what vitamins you take, or how cool you are, anyone at any age can get cancer. It doesn't discriminate.

4. You can survive. You can make it. Hang in there.
5. If you need help, ask for it. That's what friends and family are for.
6. Ask God to help you through it. Sometimes He gives the hardest battles to His strongest soldiers.
7. You will question why you, a really nice person and contributing member of society, have to put up with this cancer crap. Realize there are certain things you will never know the answer for, and this is one of them.
8. Remember, love conquers a lot, and to thank those you love, and often, for what they do for you.
9. Learn life lessons from your experience, and pass it on. You can't help others get through similar experiences unless you realize the important truths God has taught you.
10. Never, ever, forget to be grateful for each day God lets you wake up. It could have turned out a lot differently.

I would like to add a special section for cancer survivors here. Although I have understood that survivorship "officially" begins after you finish cancer treatment, I believe it begins the moment you get a cancer diagnosis. Especially in the first two years after treatment, but even for years afterwards, you will find that you have niggling doubts about your health. Listen to them. Go have that strange lump or never ending fatigue (which can last for 10 YEARS after treatment) checked out. Cancer is a chronic disease, which means it is now with you for life. Once you have one kind of cancer, you are often more prone to get others. Yes, you have survived this cancer, but be vigilant. Remember to do follow-up testing, have routine cancer screenings done, and for goodness sakes, take care of yourself already. Eat right, watch stress, and get enough sleep and exercise.

As a survivor, you will find yourself asking why. Why me? Why did it cost so much? Why do I still feel so tired? Why am I so depressed? Well, why not me? In my case, about one in eight women get breast cancer at some point in their lives. Maybe God chose me because He knew with His help I could use the cancer experience to help others. Since I had the breast cancer diagnosis, seven other women, maybe even some I really love and care about, will be spared. It is all about attitude. I try to have a daily attitude of gratitude. At least two, maybe three, of the women I got to know in my chemo group didn't survive their cancer. I still struggle with why I was spared and not them, but again, God has a plan.

Before, during, and after cancer treatment, you will experience anger, maybe a little, maybe a whole lot. My advice to you is to channel that anger. Do something productive. Fight back. There are a lot of ways to do this. My family and I chose to work for the American Cancer Society and raise funds for them every year at our community's annual Relay for Life. The first year Chris was sick, about fifty or more members of our church turned out to help raise money. We sold barbeque sandwiches, sold memorial candles, and marched to help the cause. In the last thirteen years, we have only missed one or two Relays. Being able to make the survivor lap (all cancer survivors are honored as they walk around a predetermined track, and then for the second lap they are joined by their caregivers) is one of the highlights of my year. Relays last from 6 pm until 6 am the next morning and are quite fun. One of my fondest memories of our first Relay is my daughter and her friends doing karaoke at two in the morning. I don't know if it would have been that funny during the daytime, but at two AM, it was hysterical.

There are plenty of other ways to fight back against cancer. If, like me, it brings back bad memories to actually visit a chemo room, then knit some hats for chemo patients and take them to the front office. Raise money for St Jude or other children's cancer centers, or ride a bike to raise money for leukemia patients. Don't trust charities? Go directly to the source. Volunteer to provide transportation for a cancer patient to chemo or radiation. Give money to scholarship funds for non-insured patients; buy a wig for someone who can't afford it. Don't let cancer win. Fight back in productive ways. When you get outside of yourself and help others, it helps in the healing process.

Speaking of healing, in my experience it takes about 5 years after cancer treatment is finished to become physically and emotionally well. Sometimes people, even close family members, don't understand this. If your hair is back, somehow, the perception is that you are totally healed. This is far from the truth. Cancer treatment is a scary process that not only leaves physical scars, but sometimes even larger emotional and mental ones. Add to that sometimes overwhelming financial burdens and you have a recipe for disaster. Don't hesitate to seek professional help if you need it to address these emotional issues. It is critical for the healing process to work through all of the problems you faced with cancer, not just the physical ones. Talk to your physician or other health care provider for a referral if you need one.

Chapter 6
Jan

*"Good people are taken away,
but no one understands..."*
~Isaiah 57:1

This is the hardest chapter yet, because cancer has caused me ongoing grief, and I mean daily, mostly aching, sometimes searing grief, that is almost inconsolable. Cancer finally got one of us. After four cases, number five lost. It was terrible. Here's how it went:

On the second day of February, I was driving in one of our retirement communities. I received a call on my cell phone from my sister. "Have you got a minute?" Of course I had a minute. I would have given her hours. I knew she had to go back to the doctor after having a chest x-ray. Things didn't sound good. They never are when you get that immediate call back from the doc. Apparently, my sister had been experiencing some postmenopausal bleeding for a few months, and was referred to a gynecologist. She had a biopsy and follow-up chest x-ray. The doctor called and pulled her back into his office immediately. When she called, she said, "I have endometrial cancer, and it has already spread to my lungs. I go to the oncologist tomorrow and we will decide on treatment." My heart just sank. Stage four. Cancer that has spread outside the confines of the organ it starts in. Particularly with metastasis to the lungs, things did not look particularly good. She said, "I guess you are not going to let me get by without going to Anderson?"

I said, "You got that right. I'm going to drag your behind down there to see what they can do for you."

She actually went back to her teaching job for a few days. Her lung function was awful. She became so short of breath, she required oxygen just to be able to talk and function. In the meantime, I called MD Anderson and

BEGGED them to get her in fast, but the first available appointment was for two weeks. Not good. In the meantime, we as a family were trying to stay with her round the clock. Her husband is in accounting, was in the middle of tax season, and the rest of us were working, but we managed to stay with her during the days, with her wonderful husband taking care of her at night. Her physical condition deteriorated rapidly. Within a couple of weeks, she was confined to home on oxygen and felt so unsteady we had to help her into the shower. It was horrible watching your only sister and best friend slowly weaken and be unable to breathe. We helped her all we could. We carried in meals, changed the bed, and did the laundry ... whatever she needed. Her sweet sons, both of whom lived out of town, came in to help their mom also. All of us were just devastated.

She had one chemo treatment, felt well enough to go back to work, and then had just a horrible night with diarrhea and stomach cramping. Within a few days, she went back to the doctor, had bad blood values, and had to be hospitalized. I made one visit with her to the doctor and saw her CT scan results. Her lung tissue at that time was almost totally encapsulated with cancer. Very, very, bad. She went into the hospital. Normal oxygen levels in the blood should be ninety percent or above on room air. Hers were seventy five percent on fifteen liters per minute of oxygen, the most oxygen that could be supplied to any patient in our local hospital. She was dying and I was watching, and it was tearing me to pieces. The intensive care nurses in our small community hospital were some of the most compassionate people I have ever met. They didn't follow the rules, allowing us to sit with her round-the-clock in intensive care. It was good. As it turned out, we needed every minute we could spend with her, because there were so few of them left. One of the intensive care nurses was trying to get her to relax, and said, "Envision someplace where you can relax and just lie there and rest."

She looks up at me and says, "I'll think about camping and beating you at ladder ball!"

One of her doctors said that she might be more comfortable and less stressed if she were on a respirator, and she and her husband agreed,

Me and the Big C

and she stayed on a respirator for a few days. At this point, the oncologist said there was very little, if any, hope of her getting better. My brother-in-law and their boys got the doctors together finally, because they were getting some mixed messages. My sister had a living will, and my brother-in-law used this to make the difficult decision to pull her off the respirator. With the correct paperwork in place, there are no legal questions about making a life decision like this, but without it, things get pretty hairy. So, my brother-in-law calls me and tells me, "We pulled her off the respirator and she WOKE UP." I know he was expecting her to die immediately, but she didn't. That girl was STRONG. The summer prior to her cancer, she, at age fifty-four, was riding her bike nine miles a day, teaching every day, and putting up garden. Her heart was strong, and so was her mind. No problems there, it was just the lungs that were bad.

My husband and I rushed to the hospital to see her, and she looked up at me and said, "What are you doing here?"

"Oh, just came in to see you."

After a day or so, she was moved over to a regular room, and my brother-in-law made another difficult decision to bring in hospice. Her last CT scan was even worse than the first, and there was virtually no viable lung tissue left. The last time she was weighed, she lost nine pounds in the course of a week. The squamous cell endometrial cancer was rare, and it was evil. She didn't stand a chance really. She was in the hospital and not doing well—actually on the respirator—when we reluctantly called off the trip to Houston. She was just physically unable to do it. I knew, but didn't want to believe, that she was dying, but the evidence was overwhelming. Even with an astronomical rate of oxygen going, she was just smothering to death, and there was nothing any of us could do except watch her and love and help her until she didn't need us anymore.

Some amazing things happen in the last few days before a person dies. Somehow, all the stuff that bugged you or you hadn't resolved becomes crystal clear and forgiven. I saw it happen with my own eyes. When you are dying, you don't have time to sweat the small stuff, and you take care of the big things. First on the agenda was taking care of her beloved husband of almost thirty-five years, Jerry. My sister taught for the State of Tennessee in a technical school for over thirty years, and could have retired. As part of her retirement package, she would be able to continue insurance benefits for her surviving spouse. She pushed, no, she demanded, that the insurance get resolved prior to her death. When she died, she had been retired maybe five days, but by Gosh, her husband had those insurance benefits. Jan made me promise that I would help look after Jerry. "He's going to need you all to help him. Promise me you will." We did. She also was able to see pictures of her newborn grandson just a couple of days before she died. She couldn't breathe, but she sure could smile. She had three darling granddaughters she adored, but this was the first grandson, and she smiled from ear to ear. The baby was beautiful and so was she. Another God-sent beautiful thing was a daughter-in-law she loved so much came to know the Lord, and that made her so thankful.

I was with her a few hours before she died. Her husband's sister, Laura, and I were helping her sit up in bed, and she said, "Girls, I'm ready to go," and she was. She was tired of struggling and feeling bad, and just didn't want to go on. I told her, "Jan, when the Lord is ready for you, He'll come to get you." He was, and He did, about two o'clock the next morning with her son and daughter-in-law by her side. I got the call after her husband arrived, and Mark and I loaded up and went to the hospital. Something in me was just compelled to tell her good bye. I have never experienced grief as sharp as touching the cool face of a loved one for the last time. It is searingly painful. We helped clean up her hospital room, throwing away evidence of sickness like oxygen masks and sponges to clean the mouth, because her husband didn't need to look at that anymore, and I didn't want to. Right in the trash they went. I was up the rest of the night, and at 6:00 in the morning, went to spend some time with my parents and brother who lived locally. We were distraught. She lived twenty-six days from the day she learned of her cancer diagnosis. It hit hard. We were survivors, or so we thought. We didn't know anything else to do but sit and cry and try to comfort each other.

I've talked a lot about answered prayers in this book. I prayed and still pray for my children and grandchildren's health, my health, and my parents' and husband's health almost every day. God has been so faithful, and we have an abundant wealth of prayer warriors in our church family and beyond. So if prayers were answered for Mom, Dad, Chris, and me, why weren't they answered for Jan? Simply put, I don't know, and may never know. I can see how people would turn against God in a situation like this, and simply think He wasn't listening or didn't care. He does care. The fact is everyone has to die sometime (unless you happen to be like Elijah the prophet in the Bible who was taken to heaven in a cloud while he was still alive). Otherwise, all of us have to go. Some of us even go twice, like Lazarus in the Bible. Can't you imagine how mad he was when Jesus raised him up after four days and pulled him out of Paradise? Can't you imagine his confusion and chagrin when he realized he was going to have to die AGAIN? Anyway, all mortals die. End of story. That is our earthly destiny. In Max Lucado's book, *TRAVELING LIGHT*, he talks about unanswered prayers.

Maybe it is okay for an older person to go, but what about a young child, teen, or young adult? Looking at the face of that is pretty ugly. What about those unanswered prayers? Do they cause us to lose our faith? Max quotes Isaiah 57:1-2: "Good people are taken away, but no one understands. Those who do right are being taken away from evil and are given peace. Those who live as God wants find rest in death." Max states that sometimes God doesn't answer prayers simply because He knows what may be in store for that person, and He doesn't want him or her to suffer any longer. God is a kind and loving God, and sometimes shows compassion when natural forces are in play. He doesn't interfere with it, He just ends it. Why do little kids die in car wrecks, get killed by abusers, and starve to death? Obviously, for some things there are evil forces in this world in play, but as for the others, I cannot tell you. What I can tell you is that God is faithful, God is good, and we may never know the answers. He knows them, though, and that just has to be good enough.

Until the very end, my sister was mentally sharp. In fact, she helped to plan her own funeral. The funeral was the most unique and magnificent tribute to anyone's life I have ever seen. For many years at the Baptist church my sister and her husband attended, they were involved in a puppet ministry. My sister had always said she wanted puppet music at her funeral, and that is exactly what she got. On a stage surrounded by quilts she had lovingly hand-stitched for nieces, nephews, and others, the puppets sang and danced her into heaven. It was the most unusual and most perfect memorial service I have ever witnessed. What a great tribute to a wonderful wife, mother, daughter, sister, friend, and child of God. It was a blessing.

You know, funerals are really the easy part. It is the lonely and sad days, weeks, and months afterwards that are so difficult. Grief is funny. It keeps rewinding all the could haves, should haves, and maybe it would have turned out different ifs…. Over and over again. Grief will literally kill you. It is something you have to deal with every day, and sometimes, even after years, it will come back and hit you right in the jaw. It never ends, but certainly lessens somewhat with time.

Here are some things my sister taught me about dying:

1. It is okay to be scared, but don't let that keep you from taking care of your loved ones.
2. You need to resolve all your unresolved issues with the people in your life before you go.
3. Give your loved ones permission to move on after you pass. It is a very important part of the healing process.
4. Have your paperwork in order and your legal ducks in a row. You may never need it, but you certainly might.
5. Tell your loved ones how much you love and appreciate them all the way to the very end.
6. When you die, it's not really over, it is just beginning again in a new dimension, and in a newer and better world.

Chapter 7
Advice from a Cancer Pro

Interestingly, cancer has been in my life from a number of perspectives. I am a cancer survivor, mother of a cancer patient, daughter of two cancer patients, and a sibling to a cancer victim. I have endured chemo, hair loss, worry, stress, and looking at the still and cold face of a loved one. Cancer has been horrible, hellish, and has nearly knocked my lights out. It has taught me lessons I would have never learned otherwise and maybe some lessons I never even wanted to learn. It has been the good, the bad, and the ugly. I hate it, but I can't dispute the good things that have come out of my life from the cancer experience. Here are some of them:

Hardship refines us and makes us better. There are life lessons that I would have never learned if it had not been for cancer treatment. Certainly, cancer can kill you, but it can't kill love. I have been blessed beyond measure with the family, friends, church, and community support that my family and I have received through our various cancer experiences. After our son was diagnosed, we couldn't go grocery shopping without having multiple people stop and ask us how he was doing and offer support. It was wonderful and restored my faith in humanity. Living in a small town has advantages and disadvantages, but knowing and caring for your neighbors in a genuinely good way is one huge advantage that can't be overlooked. When I was going through cancer treatment, we were supported hugely by our church family by prayers, food, money, or whatever we needed. They had our backs, and we couldn't have been gladder. My patients were as kind to me as they could be and never complained about me having to miss work occasionally for chemo, or later, surgery. My parents and siblings have been super supportive and have been the glue that held me together through the hard times and the good times as well.

Have I had blessings? Certainly. You want to know the main one? I'M ALIVE! God has spared my life for now. The Bible says all your days are numbered, and God knows this from the beginning. I take every day as a blessing now, and try not to take anything for granted. If I wake up in the morning, I thank God for another day of life. As I go to bed, or throughout the day, I thank Him for good health and safety. Instead of having bad hair days, I remember no hair days, and am thankful. Every day is a good day when you've made it, whether there are circumstances in it that are to your liking or not. I am living with an attitude of gratitude. Thanks be to God for every day.

Cancer has been a learning journey. It has been a long, difficult, trip, but like riding a long way on a real road trip, it has taken me to a beautiful place. I am so in love with my husband now, much more so than when we married thirty-five years ago. Cancer has shaped and formed him, too. Can you imagine the thought of possibly losing your child and your spouse to the same disease? How awful. He has been faithful and totally kind to me and always supportive. Divorce rates are really high among women with breast cancer. Some men hear the diagnosis and hit the road. Not my guy. He was with me every step of the way and super supportive. I know that leaving never even crossed his mind, even when I would cry and be not very lovable. He is awesome, and I am glad that he is my forever guy. He is the one for me.

Good things come out of crises if you only look for the silver lining in the cloud. Our daughter Beki has chosen to go to nursing school, and now has an advanced nursing degree. She works as a nurse practitioner in a local oncology clinic. I know that cancer has influenced not only her choice of vocation, but also the way she treats her patients and fellow man. She is a great wife, a great mom, and I am super proud of what she's accomplished. She is a faithful churchgoer, but more importantly, takes her faith outside church walls and helps her fellow man in matter-of-fact, quiet ways. She is loving and gentle, and is a great worker for the Lord.

My gentle giant, put-mother-on-the-ceiling son, is surviving cancer daily, and living his life to the fullest. He is a great employee, good

Me and the Big C

husband, and wonderful new father. He is a faithful worker in his church, and talks to the Lord on a daily basis. What a joy he has been, and I am so glad his journey is not over.

Chapter 8

A Great Day

I can't write a book about cancer without emphasizing the importance of faith. For me personally, I just would not have made the cancer trip without the Lord. It isn't good to make any trip without the Lord in your life, but it is just downright impossible to survive cancer without Him.

Starting with my son's illness in 2000 and ending with my sister's illness and death in 2010, God has had an important—no, critical—part in this journey. Interestingly, the only way you can come to terms with death is to come to terms with life—what is important to you, whom you love, what you feel for others, what your vocation is, what meaning your life has. These are all things that you have to have your heart tell you before you can come to terms with letting go. Coming to terms with death for me was a heartfelt journey. I had to reexamine what was important, and to me that was God and my relationship with Him. I for years was a faithful church member, doing unto others as I would have them do unto me, but having cancer brought me into a whole new relationship with God and his Son. Ultimately, I had to come to the conclusion that as with my son, if I died from the disease, I would be okay. Yes, at age forty-four, I would miss a lot. Seeing my kids fully raised, seeing them graduate from college, get married—these things I would miss if I would move beyond this earth's borders. I didn't cross over, and I'm glad I didn't miss these things, but if I had, I would still like to think that my life had meaning and influence beyond just an existence of a brown-eyed Tennessee farm girl. As I look back on my life, ten years away from the cancer experience, I know that even now, my life has had meaning, and I have been able to influence my husband, children, and the people around me for God. I really am glad about that. A gentleman in my hometown once spoke these words at the funeral of his brother's wife: "If you live your life and when you leave, your family, friends, and faith are intact, you have had a good life." I hope these words can be spoken about me someday, either in the near future, or many years from now. I hope that my words, actions, and my very being can positively influence the people around me.

When my son was in the first stages of his recovery, he was listening to a country music singer, Travis Tritt. The song was "It's a Great Day to be Alive." He said, "Mom, I want this to be my theme song." It's a GREAT DAY to be ALIVE. It was and it is. Blessings to all those who read this book, and may your journey in life take you to heaven.

Epilogue

In May 1985, Dr. Gordy Klatt started the first Relay for Life when he ran for twenty four straight hours to raise money for cancer awareness, research, and treatment. From that humble beginning in Tacoma Washington, the Relay for Life fundraiser has spread to large and small communities throughout the United States.

The Relay for Life, the American Cancer Society's major fundraiser, is held yearly across the country to raise money for local programs, education, and scholarships for cancer patients. A full forty percent of funds raised by the ACS goes to support cancer research.

Readers, please consider contributing to this worthy cause with money or time as a volunteer. Research and education help everyone. A portion of profits from this book will be given to my local Relay for Life team. To find Relay for Life fundraisers in your areas go to www.cancer.org or contact your local cancer center for information. Please take up the fight to stamp out cancer!

Acknowledgements

The list of people I have to thank for helping me give birth to my book is quite lengthy. First of all, hats off to Tom Bird and his staff for giving me the privilege of learning how to put my sometimes scattered thoughts down on paper and finally getting them in an organized fashion all in one spot. Tom and his staff's encouragement has been invaluable, and has finally allowed me to check one more item off my bucket list—writing a book!

Many thanks to all of the loving and competent health care providers that assisted me and all members of my family with the health issues associated with their cancer treatments. Oncology people are some of the most kind, compassionate, and loving professionals I have ever been privileged to meet. Ya'll keep up the good work!

My dear mother and father, Bud and Ella Wilson, and son, Chris Burris are also to be commended for being the inspiration to write this book, and for allowing me to share their stories.

My daughter, Beki Hillis, has been not only been my cheerleader and confidant, but also supportive of me and my efforts from the get go, and has never failed to back me up in matters of health or anything else.

My husband, Mark Burris, has been, as always, an encourager, supporter, and my biggest fan. I could not have completed this project without his utter and complete support of my vision and story of survivorship.

Even though she is no longer with us, my sister deserves a big thank you for teaching me how to live, and also, how to bravely die. I love you Sis.

Lastly, all thanks be to God, and all the glory be given to Him for the writing and inspiration for this book. I simply could not have done it without His loving grace.

About the Author

Sue Burris is a self- proclaimed Tennessee farm girl who has experienced cancer from the unique perspective of being a patient, parent, child, and sibling, all within a ten year time frame. Sue and her husband Mark, live and work on a small farm in East Tennessee and raise beef cattle and hay in addition to working jobs outside the farm.

A physical therapist for over 30 years, Sue has been a caregiver for people of all ages, and has worked in a multitude of different healthcare settings during her career, including hospitals, outpatient clinics, school systems, home health, and most recently, skilled nursing facilities. As a member of her local medical community, she has experienced health care from both a provider and patient perspective, and has used her cancer experience to mentor her patients, family, and friends with insights from her own cancer journey.

Me and the Big C is not just a book about cancer, but also about fear, heartache, and God's great love for us. Readers are encouraged to share this book with family, friends, and especially anyone they know that may be struggling with cancer. Hope is in the reading.

www.ingramcontent.com/pod-product-compliance
Lightning Source LLC
Chambersburg PA
CBHW031653040426
42453CB00006B/289